D1796496

LET'S EXPLORE THE SOIL!

By Nicole Horning

Cavendish Square

New York

Published in 2021 by Cavendish Square Publishing, LLC
243 5th Avenue, Suite 136, New York, NY 10016

Copyright © 2021 by Cavendish Square Publishing, LLC

First Edition

No part of this publication may be reproduced, stored in a retrieval system, or transmitted in any form or by any means—electronic, mechanical, photocopying, recording, or otherwise—without the prior permission of the copyright owner. Request for permission should be addressed to Permissions, Cavendish Square Publishing, 243 5th Avenue, Suite 136, New York, NY 10016. Tel (877) 980-4450; fax (877) 980-4454.

Website: cavendishsq.com

This publication represents the opinions and views of the author based on his or her personal experience, knowledge, and research. The information in this book serves as a general guide only. The author and publisher have used their best efforts in preparing this book and disclaim liability rising directly or indirectly from the use and application of this book.

All websites were available and accurate when this book was sent to press.

Cataloging-in-Publication Data
Names: Horning, Nicole.
Title: Let's explore the soil! / Nicole Horning.
Description: New York : Cavendish Square, 2021. | Series: Earth science explorers | Includes index.
Identifiers: ISBN 9781502656377 (pbk.) | ISBN 9781502656391 (library bound) | ISBN 9781502656384 (6 pack) | ISBN 9781502656407 (ebook)
Subjects: LCSH: Soils–Juvenile literature.
Classification: LCC S591.3 H687 2021 | DDC 631.4–dc23

Editor: Nicole Horning
Copy Editor: Nathan Heidelberger
Designer: Rachel Rising

The photographs in this book are used by permission and through the courtesy of: Cover Madlen/Shutterstock.com; p. 5 249 Anurak/Shutterstock.com; p. 7 Wstockstudio/Shutterstock.com; p. 9 13Imagery/Shutterstock.com; p. 11 Thai Tea/Shutterstock.com; p. 13 J. Helgason/Shutterstock.com; p. 15 Khadi Ganiev/Shutterstock.com; pp. 17, 19 Dahlhaus Kniese/Shutterstock.com; p. 21 Bukhta Yurii/Shutterstock.com; p. 23 Jurga Jot/Shutterstock.com.

Some of the images in this book illustrate individuals who are models. The depictions do not imply actual situations or events.

CPSIA compliance information: Batch #CS20CSQ: For further information contact Cavendish Square Publishing LLC, New York, New York, at 1-877-980-4450.

Printed in the United States of America

Find us on

CONTENTS

What Is Soil?

Soil is the top part of Earth that we can see and walk on. It's important to people, animals, and plants. Soil has layers, or different parts that lie on top of each other.

Soil is mostly made up of two kinds of matter. These are bits of rock and organic matter. Organic matter is something that was once alive. Most soil has many kinds of rocks and types of organic matter in it.

Parts of plants are one kind of organic matter. Sometimes there are parts of seeds, leaves, and roots in soil. If a plant has rotted a lot, it turns into a softer type of soil. This soil is dark and stays wet.

Another type of soil is light, dry, and easy to dig in. This is a sandy type of soil. It's hard for most plants to grow in sandy soil.

Soil Layers

Earth has different layers of soil called soil horizons. Each layer of soil has a different **texture**, color, and size. There are three main layers of soil. They can be seen if you look at the side of a large piece of soil.

Scientists name the main layers A, B, and C. Layer O sits on the A horizon. It's organic matter that's made up of the remains of leaves or twigs. Some areas don't have this layer. Layer R is called bedrock, which is the hard rock under the soil.

The A horizon is called topsoil. The soil is dark and soft. Under this layer is the B horizon. This is called subsoil. It's often made up of mostly clay. This soil isn't as soft as topsoil and has less organic matter in it.

17

The C horizon is called parent material. This is because it's mostly made up of pieces of rock that the rest of the soil formed from. **Weathering** hasn't changed this layer as much as the top layers of soil.

What Soil Does

Many living things make their homes in soil. Ants, beetles, worms, and groundhogs live in soil. Soil is important for them, and they are important for the soil. They help mix matter in the soil and make the soil healthier.

Soil is important for plants. It helps hold their roots so plants can stay in the ground. Soil gives plants the **nutrients** they need to grow. When it rains, soil takes in water, which plants also need to grow.

nutrients: Things needed for healthy growth.

scientists: People who study the world and how it works.

texture: The feel of an object.

weathering: Wearing away or changing something, often by air or water.